The Rural England of A. R. Quinton

Betchworth, Surrey

The River Wye at Hay-on-Wye, Herefordshire

THE RURAL ENGLAND OF A. R. QUINTON

Bygone scenes from the brush of a country artist

Carhampton, Somerset

SALMON

Published by
J Salmon Limited
100 London Road, Sevenoaks, Kent TN13 1BB

First Impression 1978
Revised edition 1990
Second Impression 1992
Third Impression 1992

Designed by the Salmon Studio

Biographical details researched by Alan Roger Quinton

ISBN 0 906198 75 5

Printed in England by
J Salmon Limited
Tubs Hill Works
100 London Road, Sevenoaks, Kent TN13 1BB

Places featured in the coloured illustrations

COTTAGE AT ELMLEY CASTLE, WORCS.

Alfred Robert Quinton

1853-1934

Alfred Robert Quinton was born on 23 October 1853, the youngest of seven children and the fifth son of John and Eliza Quinton. His parents, who had married in 1840, originally came from Suffolk; his father was born in Needham Market and his mother in Ipswich. In 1850 they moved from Ipswich to London, first to Dalston and later to Commercial Road, Peckham, where Alfred was born. John Quinton, who was both a Liberal and a staunch Congregationalist, worked on the staff of the Religious Tract Society and became Editor of the Society's publications, including *The Leisure Hour* and *The Sunday at Home;* the Society is better known for *The Boys' Own Paper* and *The Girls' Own Paper* which it also published. The influence on Quinton of his father, who did not die until March 1906 at the age of eighty-eight, was considerable, and Alfred also became a Liberal and a regular worshipper at the Congregational Church in Finchley when he settled there.

As a boy Quinton attended Hornsey School in North London. The school's headmaster was C P Newcombe whose influence was one of the main reasons for Quinton setting out on his artistic career. In July 1868, as a prize for hard work, he presented the young Alfred, then only fourteen, with a handsome leatherbound book written by George Barnard and entitled *Drawing from Nature; a series of progressive instruction in sketching from elementary studies to finished views with examples from Switzerland and the Pyrenees to which are appended lectures on art delivered at Rugby School.* This Quinton kept for the rest of his life.

After studying at Heatherley's Art School he started work as an engraver in London but soon took up painting seriously. Although he later devoted himself to watercolours and black and white drawings, he first concentrated on oils, signing himself as A Quinton, and subsequently as ARQ or AR Quinton. His last-known oil painting is dated 1885. One of his early framed oils, that of 'Great Tangley Manor, Wonersh, Surrey', painted in about 1875, remains with the family. Another large canvas entitled 'Above Wharfedale, Yorkshire', was exhibited at

The Green, Groombridge, Kent

the Imperial Jubilee Exhibition at Liverpool in 1887. From 1874 onwards Quinton was a regular exhibitor at various London societies and galleries. He first exhibited work at the Royal Academy in 1879. This was a watercolour entitled 'At Gomshall, Surrey' and, although not a member of the Academy, Quinton's pictures subsequently appeared there with regularity; twenty in all until 1919. In addition to this, between 1874 and 1893, he exhibited eighteen watercolours at the Royal Society of British Artists, nine at the New Watercolour Society, later to become the Royal Institute, one at the Grosvenor Gallery, and nine at various other exhibitions.

Until 1880 Quinton's studio was at 10 Bolt Court, Fleet Street, London, but in that year he moved to 12 New Court, Lincoln's Inn. This he shared with Henry Bailey, an artist of Quinton's age, who specialized in watercolour landscapes. Bailey's painting flourished between 1879 and 1907, and among his best works were 'The Dart at Staverton', 'Cornfield by the Sea' and 'On the Cliffs'.

As well as working in London Quinton also travelled widely throughout Europe collecting many sketches and lantern slides. He took particular pleasure in his trips to Spain in the early 1880s and it was while returning by ship from a visit to Malaga that he met his future wife, Elizabeth Annie Crompton, whom he married at Bolton, Lancashire on 20 May 1885. Annie was a descendant of Samuel Crompton, inventor of the 'mule' used for weaving. The couple went to live with Quinton's parents in Holloway before moving, after his mother's death in 1886, to 48 Fortis Green Road, East Finchley, taking with them their baby son Leonard, born on 5 March 1886, and Quinton's father. From here Quinton travelled daily by train to keep regular hours at his studio in London. In 1890 he purchased another house, lower down Fortis Green Road, and converted one room into a separate studio. However, he continued to use his New Court Studio, which his son recalled visiting in 1896, until about 1905, after which he worked solely from home. In 1891 Quinton's second son, Edgar, was born but, affected by a persistently weak heart, he died young in 1912. Not long before his death the Quintons had moved again to Westfield, Salisbury Avenue, Church End, Finchley, which was then still among fields; this large, eleven-roomed house remained with the Quinton family until 1974.

From the 1880s on Quinton was writing of his travels in England and abroad, illustrating his articles whenever possible, and slowly consolidating his reputation as an artist. 'Land's End to John o'Groats' was serialized from 4 May to 12 October 1895 in the *Illustrated Sporting and Dramatic News,* and was later published, although in less detail, in *The Leisure Hour* of 1899 and 1900. The article recounts the story of a journey undertaken on bicycles by Quinton and 'friend B' (possibly Henry Bailey) in 1894 and typifies in its text and illustrations Quinton's approach to his work, 'Our idea', he wrote, 'was to tour leisurely from end to end, to enjoy the varied scenery which our native land presents in such variety to those who care to see it, and to study the life and character which we might meet with on the road.'

This kind of journey, accompanied by a friend, was similar to many that Quinton made during his lifetime, and reflected the Victorian desire to travel and to see the world for oneself. P H Ditchfield, for whose book *The Cottages and Village Life of Rural England* (published 1912) Quinton provided seventy-one illustrations, recalled, 'We have explored together some of the quaint nooks and corners, the highways and byways, of old England, and with the pen and brush described them as they are at the present time. We have visited the peasant in the wayside cottage . . . entered the old village shop, and even taken our ease at an inn'. Quinton would be away from home for up to three months a year, staying at lodgings and farmhouses, and travelling by bicycle. He would usually work from one place for about two to three weeks at a time, and his son recalled spending enjoyable summer holidays 'on location' with his mother and father, the whole family seeing the countryside by bicycle.

High Street, Clovelly, North Devon

During the autumn, winter and spring, Quinton worked hard at Westfield in his studio, a spacious first-floor room overlooking the garden. His paintings, now all in watercolour, were worked up from numerous photographs, sketches, and drawings produced on his travels of the previous summer. He took many of his own photographs but purchased hundreds more.

Many of Quinton's watercolours were used as illustrations in magazines and books, including another of P H Ditchfield's works, *The City Companies of London and their Good Works*, published in 1904. In 1902 he illustrated articles on the Wye Valley and Wharfedale in the *Art Journal*. Of particular importance however, was a lavish book, published by Dent in 1907, entitled *The Historic Thames*. This was written by Hilaire Belloc and contained fifty-nine illustrations by Quinton. These included views of Lambeth Palace, Tower Bridge, the Houses of Parliament, Hampton Court Palace and Windsor Castle. Quinton had devoted the summers of 1905 and 1906 to work on these paintings, and the best of the originals were exhibited in 1912 at the Suffolk Street Gallery, home of the Royal Society of British Artists. The Duke and Duchess of York bought two of these pictures for their private collection. In 1907, in addition to *The Historic Thames*, a much smaller book, *Summer Holidays* by Percy Lindley, which contained a number of illustrations by Quinton, appeared. In 1910 Methuen published *The Avon and Shakespeare Country* with thirty-five illustrations by Quinton, including pictures of Shakespeare's Birthplace, Anne Hathaway's Cottage and the Vale of Evesham. At about this time a small number of paintings were published as postcards, notably a series of village crosses by Raphael Tuck & Sons.

Martyr's Worthy near Winchester, Hampshire

As well as contributing to published works Quinton was producing a large number of watercolours, many of which were commissioned and sold privately. Whereas in the 1870s and 1880s he was rarely able to sell his paintings for more than fifteen guineas apiece, by 1920 his larger pictures, approximately four feet by five feet, would fetch about one hundred guineas. He obtained some recognition for all this work when, in February 1911, he was elected a member of the Royal Society for the Encouragement of the Arts, Manufactures and Commerce.

Although he illustrated many books and booklets during the 1890s and early 1900s Quinton gained more general recognition and completed the bulk of his artistic work, in terms of pure

Goodrich Castle from the River Wye, Herefordshire

volume, through his association with J Salmon (from 1930 J Salmon Ltd), Printers and Art Publishers of Sevenoaks, Kent, from about 1912 until his death in 1934.

The printing and publishing of coloured postcards by J Salmon Ltd, Sevenoaks, Kent, dates back to the beginning of the twentieth century. In 1898 Mr Joseph Salmon had inherited control of the family printing and stationery business and, mainly through a personal interest in photography, about 1900 he began tentatively to publish black and white reproductions of photographs of the Sevenoaks neighbourhood as postcards. He soon realized that coloured postcards would have greater appeal and towards the end of 1903 the first cards were issued, reproduced from watercolour paintings by the three-colour halftone letterpress process. In 1912 an extension to the original general printing works was built in The Shambles, Sevenoaks, especially for postcard production.

Up to about 1912 various artists had been commissioned to paint pictures of their own localities and sometimes to go further afield. Although these commissions resulted in many good series, there was a lack of uniformity in the paintings, particularly when artists were working in areas with which they were unfamiliar.

It was about this time, however, that Mr Salmon, while on a visit to Selfridges Store in London, noticed on display in the art department some watercolour paintings of cottage and country scenes. He was immediately struck by the quality of the drawing, the clean, natural colouring and the generally pleasing effect that the artist had obtained. On examination he found that they were mainly country scenes in Worcestershire and that the artist's signature was AR Quinton. He was so impressed that he bought six of these pictures and, having made arrangements with the artist about the copyright, reproduced them as postcards. This small series proved so successful that it formed the foundation of an association between artist and publisher that lasted until Quinton's death in 1934, when he was eighty-one years of age and still painting. The exact date of the start of the association is unknown but 1911 would seem to be the most likely year for the Selfridges' occurrence; certainly no Quinton illustrations appear on calendars produced by the firm before those published for 1914, which would have been printed in 1913.

Having proved that the public liked the Quinton postcards, the problem was expansion. With some diffidence Mr Salmon asked Quinton if he would be willing to accept commissions to paint series of pictures of different holiday resorts and tourist areas, selecting scenes that would be attractive as postcards. After a little hesitation Quinton agreed to try the idea and soon a number of good series was being completed; views of Eastbourne, Bournemouth, Ilfracombe, Folkestone, Dover, Lynton, Brighton and Hastings, with their surrounding areas, followed one another in quick succession.

It was soon evident that Mr Salmon could commission as much of this work as Quinton could manage to undertake and, fortunately for the publisher, Quinton was willing to give it the bulk of his time. However, the outbreak of war in 1914 with, in due course the introduction of security regulations which forbade sketching in many coastal areas, threatened to put a stop to Quinton's postcard painting. In order to prevent this it was decided to make up a programme of work in areas not subject to these restrictions. Although postcards of many of these places did not have large sales, nevertheless it ensured continuity of production until 1919 when it was possible to work freely again.

Quinton's postcard work was devoted almost entirely to scenes in England and Wales although once he did cross the border into Scotland to produce a set of twelve paintings of Edinburgh. Also there was one trip abroad when he went to Ostend in 1922 to paint a set of twelve views. On this trip he was accompanied by Mr Norman Salmon who went to take photographic views of Ostend and Bruges. Thus the association continued all through the 1920s, with a slowing up after 1930, the inevitable result of Quinton's age.

A list dated 28 December 1922 details thirty-seven subjects in hand and in 1924, the peak year, an astonishing one hundred and forty-three paintings were delivered. In 1934, Quinton's last year, forty-seven commissioned works were produced, including one unfinished picture which was actually on his easel as he left it the day before he died. This last picture was a view of Sidmouth from Peak Hill in Devon (no. 4058) and was later completed by C T Howard, another artist who was working for the company at the time (the payment to the executors was accordingly reduced by thirty shillings). In all Quinton produced approximately two thousand watercolour paintings for Salmon postcards, including 1,080 known originals between December 1921 and his death. The company holds all the receipts for Quinton's paintings from this date and these show that he was paid four pounds for each painting up to November 1922, when the fee was increased to five guineas each for most of the paintings. A lesser fee was sometimes paid if the painting did not include any figures. Also a number of originals were altered by the artist from time to time according to the changing demands of the market.

The range of Quinton's artistic skill was extraordinary. He produced paintings not only of his favourite cottages and villages but a continuous succession of all types of local-view subject matter – piers, promenades and gardens, beaches and boating lakes, castles and cathedrals, mountains and waterfalls, cliffs and harbours – any picture that was required and all in an inimitable style that raised even the most prosaic and uncompromising scene from the rut of purely representational art. In this he stood head and shoulders above artists working for other publishers in the same period, none of whom ever captured Quinton's universal appeal – many tried, but not one of them came anywhere near him.

As a person Quinton, bearded and well known in later years for his grey Homburg hat and bunch tie, was a kindly man,

King John's Bridge, Tewkesbury, Gloucestershire

purposeful yet quiet, talking little about his work. Although he could be disagreeable when angry, he was fair and strict as a father, was not a lover of socializing and had a very limited circle of friends, preferring to mix with his family. Leonard and his wife Nellie visited Westfield with their children every Sunday at 4 pm for tea, and Quinton was also very close to his elder brother Ernest, the manager of a large City jewellers. He only discarded his favourite tweed jacket for occasional Royal Academy dinners and for the regular Sunday attendance at the Congregational Church where he sang with a fine bass voice. He often smoked a briar pipe, or an occasional cigar, even when working, but was not given to drinking, the infrequent whisky being taken from a porcelain decanter on the sideboard. His favourite pastimes were gardening and carpentry, and he kept a workshop where he did much of his own picture framing. He tended the large lawn, trees, and flowerbeds at Westfield with care, and so loved the peace of the garden that, so the story goes, while Leonard was away in France during the First World War, he created a small flowerbed in the centre of the lawn to ensure that the lawn could no longer be used for tennis and cricket.

In his painting Quinton's particular gift was his ability to capture the flavour and colour of English rural life at the turn of the century. This he achieved, especially in his earlier water-colours, in several ways. First, through his skill as a draughts-man he could reproduce accurately and in great detail the subject before him, and yet his paintings are never dull, 'photographic' images. He avoided this partly through his rich and varied use of colour, and partly through the clever manner in which he composed his pictures. He made continual use of distinctly rural elements, such as herds of cattle, flocks of sheep, horses and carts, and standing or seated figures, all of which consistently appear throughout his work, not only to bring his paintings to life, but also to suggest the air of tranquillity which he was trying to evoke. It was this ability to combine accuracy with an impression of rural peace and harmony which made Quinton's watercolours so popular as postcards although, due mainly to the volume of work he undertook and advancing years, his later

Keeper's Cottage, Hindhead, Surrey

Brandish Street near Porlock, Somerset

work lacks something of the original quality and freshness.

The essence of Quinton's appeal is therefore mainly nostalgic. Although he did produce many town and coastal views for postcards, he derived greatest pleasure from painting village and country scenes, thatched and half-timbered cottages being his favourite theme. In particular he was very concerned to leave a record of rural England in case it should ever be destroyed. P H Ditchfield, with whom Quinton collaborated in 1904 and 1912, wrote:

> 'Agitators are eager to pull down our old cottages and erect new ones which lack all the grace and charm of our old-fashioned dwellings. It is well to catch a glimpse of rural England before the transformation comes, and to preserve a record of the beauties that for a time remain.'

During Quinton's long association with Mr Joseph Salmon and his company, which lasted over twenty years, there grew up a friendship between the two men, and Mr and Mrs Quinton made visits to Mr and Mrs Salmon at their home in Sevenoaks on a number of occasions. Both Mr Joseph Salmon and his son Mr Norman Salmon personally attended the funeral, after which they collected the final paintings from the studio. Thus was closed a unique chapter in the story of postcard publication, though the wide appreciation of Quinton's work continues undiminished through the many publications issued by J Salmon Limited year by year.

THE VILLAGE CROSS, RIPPLE, WORCESTERSHIRE

The charming timber, tile and brick village of Ripple near the River Severn centres round the green with its slender cross. The 12th century church is famous for its finely preserved 15th century carved stalls and misericordes.

VILLAGE CROSS
RIPPLE Nr TEWKESBURY

A MILL ON THE RIVER GIPPING, SUFFOLK

Rising deep in the Suffolk countryside, the River Gipping flows through Stowmarket and Needham Market to join the Orwell at Ipswich. It was canalised by 15 locks to serve the rural communities along its banks but is no longer navigable.

A.R.Q

LITTLE COMBERTON, WORCESTERSHIRE

Among the most attractive villages of the Vale of Evesham, Little Comberton lies on the lower slopes of Bredon Hill. Its timber-framed, thatched cottages and stone-walled gardens are overlooked by the 500 year old tower of St. Peter's Church.

A.R. QUINTON

THE CROWN INN, GROOMBRIDGE, KENT

Standing on the border of Kent and Sussex the picturesque village of Groombridge is renowned for 'The Walks', a charming row of brick, tiled and weatherboarded cottages with the Crown Inn overlooking the triangular green.

PRSA

ARUNDEL CASTLE, WEST SUSSEX

The ancient fortress of Arundel Castle towers with medieval splendour high above the River Arun where it cuts through a gap in the South Downs. The castle owes its present outline to extensive rebuilding carried out during the 19th century.

A.R.QUINTON

THE FORD, KERSEY, SUFFOLK

The picturesque and unspoilt village of Kersey, which prospered on the medieval wool trade, has colour-washed and half-timbered houses lining its single street which runs steeply down to a shallow watersplash. Its church has a fine flint tower.

A.R. QUINTON

A COTTAGE AT GARSINGTON, OXFORDSHIRE

A few miles to the south-east of Oxford, in a fine sweeping countryside, is delightful Garsington, a village with an old cross, a 16th century manor house with remarkable yew hedges and a church with a fine Norman tower.

UINTON
GARSINGTON NR OXFORD

THE VALE OF EVESHAM, WORCESTERSHIRE

Between Pershore and Tewkesbury Shakespeare's River Avon winds in great serpentine loops around the distinctive bulk of Bredon Hill which dominates the river and gives wonderful views across the Vale of Evesham to the distant Malvern Hills.

THE BRIDGE, COOMBE BISSETT, WILTSHIRE

Standing on the banks of the little River Ebble as it flows to join the Wiltshire Avon, the pretty village of Coombe Bissett with its stone bridge and old church beside the road lies a short distance to the south west of Salisbury.

COOMBE BISSETT
Nr SALISBURY
A.R.QUINT

SONNING, BERKSHIRE

Charming Sonning village contains a wealth of old houses and colourful gardens, a mill and a church with a fine screen and several interesting brasses. The Deanery, in a garden designed by Gertrude Jekyll, is a good example of Lutyens's style.

A.R.Q.

HAMPTON FERRY, RIVER AVON, WORCESTERSHIRE

A short way downstream from Evesham, in the heart of the Worcestershire fruit and vegetable growing district, this unusual hand operated ferry carries foot passengers across the River Avon on the edge of the little village of Hampton.

A.R.Q.
HAMPTON FERRY. EVESHAM

THE BARLEY MOW, CLIFTON HAMPDEN, OXFORDSHIRE

At Clifton Hampden, a quaint secluded village with a pretty church standing on a cliff and a fine brick bridge over the River Thames, stands the ancient Barley Mow Inn, built with massive oaken crucks supporting its thatched roof.

A.R.Q.
THE BARLEY MOW INN
CLIFTON HAMPDEN, OXON.

THE VILLAGE CROSS, EAST HAGBOURNE, OXFORDSHIRE

East Hagbourne, formerly in Berkshire, is one of the prettiest of villages with its old cottages of timber, tile and thatch surrounded by pretty gardens, an ancient slender-shafted cross and a church with a splendid carved medieval roof.

LEEDS CASTLE NEAR MAIDSTONE, KENT

There can be no more romantically situated building in all England than Leeds Castle near Maidstone whose venerable stone walls rise directly from the waters of an enchanted lake surrounded by gently sloping grassy banks.

LEEDS CASTLE, Nr MAIDSTONE
A.R.QUINTON

THE CROSS, CASTLE COMBE, WILTSHIRE

Castle Combe, nestling in a deep wooded valley on the southern edge of the Cotswolds, is a village of lovely old cottages grouped around a stone roofed market cross and lining the single narrow street to the bridge.

A.R.QUINTON

A FORD NEAR WIXFORD, WARWICKSHIRE

Near the village of Wixford this pretty summer evening scene of an old cottage, a rustic bridge and shallow watersplash across a brook, a tributary of the little River Arrow, epitomises the peaceful charm of Shakespeare's countryside.

THE HARBOUR, NEWLYN, CORNWALL

Westwards from Penzance and overlooking Mount's Bay is the old fishing village of Newlyn, beloved haunt of artists. This quaint place possesses a horse-shoe shaped harbour which invariably presents a gay and busy scene.

A.R. QUINTON

THE DORSET ARMS, HARTFIELD, EAST SUSSEX

Between the elevated heathland of Ashdown Forest and the fertile River Medway valley lies Hartfield, a village street of brick, timber and tile-hung cottages, old inns and a church with a curious lychgate and a shingled spire.

THE DORSET ARMS INN
HARTFIELD, SUSSEX
A.R.Q.

BUCKLAND, SURREY

Tiny Buckland with its green, old cottages and barns and reed-fringed pond is but one of the number of pretty villages that are strung out like jewels beneath the line of the North Downs between Reigate, Dorking and Guildford.

BUCKLAND NR REIGATE
A.R.QU

CROPTHORNE HILL, WORCESTERSHIRE

Standing near the River Avon, attractive Cropthorne has largely grown up around its single street. It comprises a pleasing variety of building styles, including a number of the black and white cottages which are so characteristic of the area.

THE TROUT INN, GODSTOW, OXFORDSHIRE

Very well known to Oxford people is the stone built riverside Trout Inn at Godstow beside a backwater of the Thames; a pleasant place at which to slake a thirst on a warm summer day. Nearby are the extant fragments of Godstow Nunnery.

THE TROUT INN, GODSTOW
UPPER THAMES

CHANCTONBURY RING, WEST SUSSEX

Behind Worthing on an escarpment of the South Downs is Chanctonbury Ring, an ancient earthwork surrounded by a fine clump of beech trees planted in 1760. Standing about 800 feet above sea level, they were sadly marred by the 1987 storm.

A.R.QUINTON

THE BOCKINGFORD ARMS, LOOSE, KENT

Set in a steep, wooded Kentish valley, Loose is a village of ups and downs, of twisting byways and hidden corners through which the little River Loose appears and disappears on its way to join the River Medway at Maidstone.

BOCKINGFORD ARMS.
OLD INN, LOOSE VALLEY,
Nr MAIDSTONE
A.R. QUINTON.

THE SHIPWAY, ROBIN HOOD'S BAY, YORKSHIRE

The wide sweep of Robin Hood's Bay on the North Yorkshire coast stretches from Ravenscar to North Cheek. The village lies in a steep-sided ravine running down to the foreshore and its older part is a maze of narrow streets.

THE SHIPWAY,
ROBIN HOOD'S BAY

COTTAGES AT ELMLEY CASTLE, WORCESTERSHIRE

Situated at the foot of Bredon Hill, the attractive little village of Elmley Castle contains a wealth of half-timbered and thatched cottages, many of which have incorporated in their fabric stones taken from the ruined Norman castle.

A.R.Q

SONNING BRIDGE, RIVER THAMES

Sonning is a Thames-side village largely hidden from the river which is here spanned by a mellow red brick bridge, one of the oldest on the river. A short way upstream is Sonning Lock, renowned for its trim and colourful garden.

A.R.QUINTON

BRAY, BERKSHIRE

Beside the Thames a short way below Maidenhead, though secluded from the river, is Bray, an attractive village which has been immortalised by the turncoat 'Vicar of Bray' whose church, dating from 1293, stands at the end of the street.

The
RINGERS
A.R.Q

SHERE, SURREY

Midway between Guildford and Dorking, the charming village of Shere is situated on the River Tillingbourne and surrounded by woodland. Old cottages are grouped around its tiny green and the church has a Norman tower with a fine shingled spire.

FRIAR'S CRAG, DERWENTWATER, CUMBRIA

Derwentwater is known as the Queen of the English Lakes with its rich blending of green fells, steep crags and feathery woods. Near Keswick is the pine-clad headland of Friar's Crag, one of Lakeland's loveliest and best known landmarks.

A.R QUINTON

THE OLD BOAR'S HEAD, BISHOP'S STORTFORD, HERTFORDSHIRE

The market town of Bishop's Stortford grew up around an 11th century castle built to guard a ford across the River Stort. It is noted as the birthplace of Cecil Rhodes founder of Rhodesia, for its College and for its fine old hostelries.

BOARS
HEAD
HOTEL
HOTEL
THE OLD BOAR'S HEAD
BISHOPS STORTFORD
A.R.QUINTON

THE SMITHY, PENSHURST, KENT

Penshurst, set above the steep sided valley of the infant River Medway, is famous for the great medieval house Penshurst Place, picturesque Leicester Square and the old smithy with its unusual horse-shoe shaped door portal.

J.E. SKINNER
A.R

NEWTON FERRERS, SOUTH DEVON

Wooded slopes rising steeply from the sheltered waters of the River Yealm provide a picturesque setting for the village of Newton Ferrers which has a narrow street running down to the estuary where many small boats bob at their moorings.

PLYMOUTH
NEWTON ON THE YEALM
A.R.QUINTON

AN OLD COTTAGE NEAR LOOE, CORNWALL

Deep in the Cornish countryside, inland from the fishing village of Looe, this delightful cottage scene of stout stone walls snugly covered by weathered thatch with the cottager tending her hens evokes the rural peace of old England.

A.R QUINTON

WYRE PIDDLE, WORCESTERSHIRE

Wyre Piddle stands astride the road from Evesham to Worcester on the high northern bank of Shakespeare's River Avon. Behind the street, with its ancient cross, the village gardens slope steeply down to the water's edge.

THE CROSS, LONG WITTENHAM, OXFORDSHIRE

Beside the Thames away from the navigable channel and within view of the distinctively shaped Sinodun Hills, or Wittenham Clumps, is the picturesque village of Long Wittenham with its ancient stone 'chipping' or market cross.

A.R.QUINTON

CHIDDINGSTONE, KENT

The tiny unspoilt village of Chiddingstone lies near the River Eden in the Weald of Kent. Lining the street, opposite the church, is a striking row of timber-framed houses behind which is the Chiding Stone from which the village takes its name.

CHIDDINGSTONE, KENT
ARQ

A COTTAGE AT HARVINGTON, WORCESTERSHIRE

The Vale of Evesham is renowned for its lovely old villages with their black and white half-timbered 16th and 17th century cottages framed with stout English oak filled with wattle, daub and brick and roofed with snug and homely thatch.

THE WHITE HART, WYTHAM, OXFORDSHIRE

Lying beneath a beautiful wooded hill within the great loop of the Thames above Oxford is Wytham, a charming village of old cottages of stone and thatch, a stone-roofed inn, and a fine Elizabethan house with a 15th century gatehouse.

THE WHITE HART INN
WYTHAM, Nr OXFORD
A.R.Q

A DEVONSHIRE LANE AT COCKINGTON

This cool, tree-shaded lane, so typical of the soft, lush countryside of South Devon, leads to the quaint hamlet of Cockington which is renowned for its ancient and picturesque thatched forge and its colour washed, cob-walled cottages.

DEVONSHIRE LANE, COCKINGTON
NR TORQUAY.
A.R.QUINTON

COTTAGES AT STEVENTON, OXFORDSHIRE

Formerly in Berkshire the village of Steventon has a very large green and a remarkable half-mile long raised and tree-lined causeway beside the street to the church around which there is a picturesque group of timbered cottages.

IBBERTON, DORSET

The sturdy cottages of Ibberton are typical of one of the most pleasant and unspoiled stretches of English countryside. On a ridge of hills to the west of Blandford Forum, the village is surrounded by secluded valleys and peaceful streams.

A.R.Q.

FRIDAY STREET, LEITH HILL, SURREY

Five miles from Dorking, under the shadow of Leith Hill, is Friday Street, a picturesque lakeside hamlet surrounded by woods. The unusually named Stephen Langton Inn recalls the cardinal who was Archbishop of Canterbury from 1207 to 1288.

A.R.QUINTON

ELMLEY CASTLE, WORCESTERSHIRE

Picturesque Elmley Castle presents a tranquil scene with black and white timbered cottages, thatched and tiled roofs and mellow brick walls. The main street, bordered by a streamlet, leads to the square and the inn with its oak-beamed interior.

.MLEY CASTLE, WORCS.

FELPHAM NEAR BOGNOR, WEST SUSSEX

The village of Felpham has a long and honourable history having belonged at one time to King Alfred; it possesses a venerable stone church dating from the early 12th century. The poet and artist William Blake once occupied a cottage here.

CHURCH
FARM
DAIRY
FELPHAM, Nr BOGNOR
A.R. QUINTON

LORNA DOONE FARM, MALMSMEAD, SOMERSET

Standing beside the bridge and ford across the Badgworthy Water on the edge of Exmoor, Lorna Doone Farm is linked with the infamous Doones and was immortalised as the home of John Ridd in R.D. Blackmore's famous novel.

LORNA DOONE FARM
MALMSMEAD

POUNDS BRIDGE NEAR PENSHURST, KENT

The hamlet of Pounds Bridge which lies enfolded in the wooded Kentish hills near Penshurst is best known for this fine half-timbered house built by William Darknoll in 1593 and whose initials are worked into the massive oak framing.

1593
POUNDS BRIDGE, NR PENSHURST
A.R.Q

LITTLE JANE'S COTTAGE, BRADING, ISLE OF WIGHT

This romantic cottage is forever linked with the story of Jane "The Young Cottager" recorded by Rev. Legh Richmond, sometime curate of Brading, in his "Annals of the Poor". She died aged fifteen in 1799 and is buried in the churchyard.

LITTLE JANE'S
COTTAGE
TEA
A.R.QUINT

THE GREEN, OCKLEY, SURREY

It would be difficult to find a scene more typically English than the green at Ockley with its village pump and cricket pitch surrounded by old cottages and venerable trees. In the distance Leith Hill rises to a height of 965 feet.

OCKLEY, Nr DORKING
A.R.QUINTON

Pretty Corner, Sheringham, Norfolk